Original title:
Tropical Reflections

Copyright © 2025 Creative Arts Management OÜ
All rights reserved.

Author: Rory Fitzgerald
ISBN HARDBACK: 978-1-80581-532-7
ISBN PAPERBACK: 978-1-80581-059-9
ISBN EBOOK: 978-1-80581-532-7

The Alchemy of Ocean and Sky

The sun and sea create a dance,
A crab in shades, takes a chance.
With flip-flops stuck in sandy glee,
It scuttles like it's lost in spree.

A coconut falls, causing a laugh,
The tourists scatter, just like the chaff.
A seagull swoops with a reckless dive,
Snatching a chip, feeling alive.

The waves are gossiping, oh so bold,
Whispers of treasures, stories retold.
With every splash, a chuckle erupts,
A fish in a tux says, "What's up, pups?"

Under the shade of a palm tree's sway,
A sunburned tourist yells, "Hey! No way!"
The ocean chuckles, laced with sun,
In this grand comedy, we laugh and run.

Memory of a Summer Rain

Raindrops dance on our heads,
Like silly hats upturned instead.
We slip and slide on puddles wide,
Wearing laughter like a tide.

A frog croaks out a cheeky tune,
While ducks parade beneath the moon.
We splash through joy, our cares all drain,
Oh, what a laugh in summer rain!

Sand Between Our Toes

Sticky toes and giggles loud,
Building castles with our cloud.
Seagulls steal our lunches fast,
While we chase waves, a wild blast.

The sun burns bright, our noses red,
Ice cream drips, a tasty dread.
The sand gets everywhere, oh dear,
But laughter's more than sand, I fear!

Calm Waters and Golden Skies

Floating on a giant tube,
The water's calm, a playful rube.
Fishes winking, what a sight,
Jumping in and out, a delight!

Golden rays bounce on our skin,
Splashing friends, let the fun begin!
With every wiggle, every shout,
We forgot what life's about!

Lost in the Lush Wilderness

We wandered deep, oh what a trip,
Chasing shadows, making quips.
A monkey giggles, hangs from trees,
While we trip over roots like clumsy bees.

A bug just landed on my nose,
But hey, that's just how it goes!
We stumble through this green parade,
In laughter's arms, we're not afraid.

Heartbeat of the Horizon

The sun wears shades, oh what a sight,
A seagull stole my sandwich, what a fright!
Waves crash in rhythm, a goofy dance,
I trip on flip-flops, lost in a trance.

Sandy toes wiggle, they've got their own beat,
Mermaids giggle as they sway and repeat.
Path of laughter, I lose my way,
Chasing crabs, they start to play!

Echoing Laughter Under the Palms

Palms sway gently, throwing shade and cheer,
A coconut drops, it's the fruit of the year!
Checkered blankets spread on the sunlit sand,
Sipping green drinks, I spill—oh, what a brand!

The ocean's a jester, it splashes and roars,
I slip on a wave and roll back to the shores.
Grinning seashells whisper secrets wide,
In this wild paradise, I take a ride!

Reflections on a Serene Shore

Mirror-like waters, fish wearing a grin,
A crab gives a wink, 'Let the games begin!'
Bouncing along with my goofy flair,
Turtles nod slowly, they just don't care.

Seashells decorate this sandy terrain,
I trip on my towel, oh, what a pain!
Laughter erupts as I tumble and roll,
Joy drips like honey, sweetens my soul!

Fragments of Coastal Tranquility

At dawn, the beach is a circus of cheer,
A dog steals my towel, haven't seen him here!
Sandcastles giggle as the tide creeps near,
I build a moat, but it disappears, dear.

In the hammock, I swing, dreaming in glee,
Why on earth did I think I could sip tea?
The waves are my audience, clapping so loud,
My beach-side performance, I'm quite the crowd!

Vibrant Horizons

Sunshine spills like pancakes wide,
Bikinis dance, an endless slide.
Coconuts fall, a drummer's beat,
Little crabs march, oh what a treat!

Flip-flops flapping, a joy to see,
Sandcastle kings, they reign with glee.
Seagulls squawking, a raucous choir,
Sunburnt noses, they never tire!

Cascades of Color

Painted skies and fruit that's bright,
Sipping smoothies, oh what a sight!
Pineapple hats, we're the strange crew,
Dancing with shadows, just me and you.

Bright flowers wink, they call our name,
Laughter echoes, it's all a game.
Hula hoops spinning, just like our fun,
Life's a beach, let's soak in the sun!

Driftwood Memories

Old surfboards drift on soft waves,
Tales of mermaids in gardens of caves.
Shells that whisper, with secrets old,
Fossilized laughter, worth more than gold.

Sticky fingers from ice cream cones,
Pickle-flavored chips, or so the gnome moans.
Chasing sunsets, what a wild ride,
Echoes of giggles, the ocean our guide!

Lush Reveries

Bamboo bends like a dancer's grace,
Mangoes wink, as if to race.
Giggling geckos in leafy veils,
Whispers of humor in breezy trails.

Parrots shout with vibrant cheer,
Pineapple jokes that only we hear.
Tropical dreams, they come alive,
In this circus, we all thrive!

Ephemeral Paradise

In a hammock, I sway and flip,
A coconut falls, oh, what a trip!
The sun's too bright, my hat takes flight,
Chasing shadows, what a sight!

Lizards dance with gusto and pride,
While I fumble, arms open wide.
A seagull steals my tasty snack,
And I'm left with an empty pack!

Moments in Color

Pineapples wear their crowns so bold,
While mangoes whisper secrets untold.
Papayas giggle in the breeze,
They twirl and spin with such great ease!

A rainbow splash of fruity cheer,
Bananas laugh as I draw near.
Behind each palm, a joke awaits,
A party hidden by the gates!

Island Echoes

Waves crash in a playful tease,
I try to dance, but fall with ease.
Crabs scuttle, joining the fun,
As the sun beams down, oh what a run!

The parrot squawks, "What's that you say?"
I toss a shell, it flies away.
Echoes of laughter mingle in air,
Chasing memories, without a care!

Beneath the Coconut Canopy

Beneath the palms, I sit with glee,
A squirrel attempts to outsmart me.
In this shade, I nap, then wake,
To find a mango in the lake!

Turtles giggle, slipping on sand,
While I balance a drink in hand.
Each splash and giggle makes me grin,
In this quirky land, I always win!

The Melody of Island Lullabies

Beneath a coconut tree, I sway,
A parrot sings, come join the play.
The waves crash softly, like a joke,
While crabs in tuxedos dance and poke.

Shells giggle on the shore so bright,
A starfish twirls, what a funny sight!
The ocean hums a silly tune,
As sunbeams dance, like cartoons.

Radiant Flora and Hidden Fauna

The flowers wear their colors bold,
A daisy's gossip starts to unfold.
While bees in suits buzz on by,
A butterfly winks, oh my oh my!

Lizards dressed in emerald green,
Practice yoga, looking serene.
A monkey drops a banana peel,
And giggles at the clumsy deal.

Echoes of Paradise

The palm trees whisper funny tales,
Of beach ball battles and joyous flails.
A turtle races with a snail,
While seagulls try to cook a pail.

In laughter, the waves rise and fall,
Fish play hide and seek, what a ball!
The sunset bursts in colorful hues,
As shadows dance in funny shoes.

Sun-Kissed Moments

With sunscreen slathered, I feel so slick,
I slip on sunshine, what a trick!
The ice cream melts, a drippy fate,
As laughter bubbles, can't be late!

A hammock sways, a cozy nest,
Where all the giggles find their rest.
The sun dips low, a golden screen,
As nightime jokes reign supreme.

Nestled in Shade

Under a palm, I nap with glee,
A coconut drops, oh woe is me!
I wake to laughter, a crab on my toe,
"Hey friend!" it squeaks, "Let's steal the show!"

Sunshine laughs, it tickles my face,
While the breeze says, "Come join the race!"
A lizard does yoga, how stretches so sleek,
I think I'll just chill, that sounds less bleak.

Secrets of the Shoreline

Shells whisper tales, of fish with wigs,
As seagulls dance, practicing jigs.
The tide rolls in, like a clumsy clown,
And crabs in tuxedos, strut up and down.

The sand giggles as it tickles my toes,
While a beach ball sails—oh where it goes!
A flip-flop army brings laughter so bold,
As the sun drops low, its warmth turns to gold.

Harmonies of Hibiscus

Flowers in hats are singing a tune,
While bees do the cha-cha under the moon.
A parrot cracks jokes, with feathers so bright,
While the blossoms just sigh, "This is pure light!"

The lilies join in, they're all in a spin,
With butterflies twirling, they let the fun win.
I've joined the rave in this flowery space,
Hibiscus giggles, this is the place!

Waves of Solitude

The ocean's a joker, splashing with flair,
It pulls at my ankles with salty cold air.
I tried to surf, but fell with a splash,
The fish all chuckled, 'Oh what a crash!'

Waves whisper secrets, while I ponder life,
A dolphin flips by, full of mischief and ripe.
I raise my hands high, a victory sign,
But it's only the seagulls that truly align.

Waves of Sunlit Dreams

The seagulls squawk, a cheeky laugh,
As beach balls bounce in crazy paths.
A crab in shorts does a little dance,
While sandcastles fall, not leaving a chance.

Flip-flops flying, just like their wearers,
Sunscreen battles, two stubborn bearers.
Kids chase waves with squeals of delight,
While wiggling worms take cover from light.

Ice cream drips down sticky hands,
Melted dreams in shifting sands.
Laughter echoes where shells have been,
As sleepy beachgoers snooze in between.

At sunset, the skies turn a shade of gold,
While a parrot squawks gossip that's bold.
With all the fun, the sun starts to hide,
But the joy of the day will forever abide.

In the Shade of Palms

Under green umbrellas, we sip our drinks,
The coconut one makes everyone think.
A sunburnt tourist wears a bright hat,
While a local cat just snickers at that.

Children giggle, playing tag with shade,
While sunbathers lie down, quite unafraid.
A lizard slips by with a sneak peek,
Under the palms, we all feel unique.

Sunscreen is splattered like art gone wrong,
With sticky hugs, we all sing along.
There's dancing bamboo with a rhythm so fine,
As we laugh at each other's silly design.

Coconuts fall, a soft thud on sand,
Bringing surprise to a day so grand.
In palm-fringed laughter, we float and glide,
With the sun on our backs, we can't help but ride.

Swaying to the Ocean's Whisper

The waves chat softly like giggling friends,
As seaweed dances while laughter blends.
With every splash, a funny surprise,
Crab antics steal the show with sly eyes.

Surfboards wobble like jelly on toes,
As wipeouts prompt laughter like comic shows.
A dolphin jumps high, a splash in the air,
While a seagull steals fries without a care.

In salty breezes, jokes float on by,
With sea turtles grinning, oh my, oh my!
Sunburns are badges of honor we wear,
As flip-flops abandon feet without a care.

At the shoreline where giggles abide,
We gather memories that cannot hide.
With whispers of waves, our laughter entwined,
The harmony of joy is perfectly timed.

Sunset Serenade

As daylight dims and colors collide,
The sun throws a party, what a joyride!
Fish splash about, doing flips and dives,
While the flip-flop band competes with live jives.

A parrot sings tunes that tickle the air,
As sunset skies flaunt their vibrant flair.
The beachcombers chuckle at sand in their hair,
While crabs in tuxedos are quite the rare fare.

When twilight arrives with a wink and a grin,
The stars start to twinkle, let the fun begin!
Shells become instruments, we laugh and play,
In this sunset serenade, we'll dance and sway.

With every note from the evening's embrace,
We share silly stories, smiles on each face.
As the moonlight dances upon the shore,
Together we revel and always want more.

Shadows Dance Among the Leaves

In the breeze, a leaf did twirl,
A sneaky bug began to swirl.
It slipped and slid on sunlit ground,
Chasing shadows all around.

A frog jumps high, but lands so wrong,
He croaks a tune, a funny song.
The sunlight winks, the branches sway,
While giggles echo through the day.

A monkey swings, he grabs a vine,
And makes a face, oh so divine!
His prankster tricks make others blush,
As laughter fills the leafy hush.

The shadows stretch, the sun slips low,
The bug now dances, steals the show.
With every flip, the forest gleams,
As laughter nests in sunny dreams.

Traces of Laughter in the Sand

On the shore, a crab does dance,
In little steps, he takes a chance.
He flips and flops, a tiny clown,
While beach balls bounce and tumble down.

A seagull circles with a gleeful squawk,
Stealing snacks like a sly hawk.
With every snack, his belly grows,
And laughter bursts as joy just flows.

Sandcastles melt from ocean's kiss,
A kid yells out, "Oh, what a mess!"
But giggles rise like ocean foam,
As waves claim back their sandy home.

The sun dips low, the day says bye,
With footprints left, just one more try.
As stars above begin to peek,
We hold the laughter, oh so sleek.

Starlit Calm

In twilight's glow, the crickets play,
Their chirps turn cheeky, hip-hip-hooray!
A firefly buzzes, with vest of light,
Flashing 'hello' with all its might.

The moon grins wide, a silver snack,
As raccoons gather, no skills they lack.
They tiptoe close, with mischief flair,
Planning heists under the starlit air.

A shadow leaps, a pup runs wild,
Here comes a chase, let's all be wild!
With barks and yaps, the evening hums,
While laughter dances, joy becomes.

The night wraps tight in cozy bliss,
A whisper of dreams, not one's to miss.
As stars above begin to shimmer,
We chuckle softly, our hearts feel warmer.

Journey Through Lush Landscapes

In the jungle's heart, a parrot squawks,
With colors bright, he plays and mocks.
He imitates all who pass by,
While jungle critters giggle, oh my!

A snake slithers, in style and grace,
But trips on roots—what a funny face!
His scales shimmer in the bright sunbeam,
As laughter bubbles, a joyful theme.

A piña colada spills with a splash,
All in laughter, no need to dash.
With drinks in hand, we toast to cheer,
As butterflies join, not showing fear.

The path ahead winds through the glee,
With every step, more fun to see.
In every leaf, in every sound,
Our journey sings, where joy is found.

Mirage of the Painted Sky

In the morning light, the sun does dance,
Clouds wear pink like a party pants.
Parrots squawk, they gossip and tease,
I trip on a sandcastle, oh dear me, please!

Lizards sunbathe, with sunglasses on,
While turtles play chess till the day is gone.
Seashells gossip, sharing their news,
Crabs salsa dance in their tiny shoes.

Waves play tag with the shores nearby,
A dolphin leaps, letting out a sigh.
The sunset's canvas turns quite absurd,
As I chuckle at the postcard blurred.

An Invitation to Surrender

The hammock sways, a gentle embrace,
Who needs a plan? Just drift in place.
Sipping coconuts, feeling so bright,
Watch out for the seagull, he's eyeing my bite!

Plumeria blooms, offering a whiff,
The breeze carries gossip, a raucous riff.
Flip-flops squeaking like a cheerful tune,
While crabs applaud under the lazy moon.

Fish in the sea wear sequined scales,
Underwater parties with bubble trails.
So let's surrender, just let it all go,
Join the parade where the sea creatures flow.

The Heart of a Hidden Lagoon

In a secret nook, a lagoon does glitter,
The frogs play poker, their bets make me twitter.
Dragonflies zoom like they own the day,
While I giggle and trip, what a silly ballet!

Lemons squeeze laughter from the palm trees,
While fish do the limbo with graceful ease.
A snorkeling snail, slow but sincere,
Winks at the world with a shell full of cheer.

Is that a mermaid, or just a flounder?
Her tail's quite the tale, I cannot expound here.
Splashing around, my worries do flee,
In this lagoon, I pretend to be free.

Turquoise Dreams

Close your eyes to the sun, take a leap,
The sea whispers nonsense, giggles so deep.
Flip-flops float by like boats made of sighs,
As jellyfish joust in inflatable ties.

The waves do a conga, a shimmering spree,
While sandcastles argue about who's the key.
Seashells collect stories, they share with a grin,
Each grain holds a treasure, a secret within.

With laughter like bubbles in warm ocean blue,
I dance with the tide, it's a whimsy debut.
Under palm tree chandeliers, we twirl around,
In the land of turquoise, silliness is found.

Island Echoes

A crab in a hat, what a sight to behold,
Dancing on sand while the sun turns to gold.
The fish gossip wildly, in bubbles they chat,
As seagulls squawk jokes, 'Hey, where's all the mat?'

A monkey in sunglasses, swinging with glee,
Found a bright coconut, declared it his tea.
He sips with a grin, oh what a nice view,
While the waves roll in, laughing hard at the crew.

A turtle with flip-flops races the breeze,
He trips on his shell, says 'Next time, I'll please!'
The laughter erupts, oh what fun in the sun,
Underneath the clear sky, everyone's on the run.

When night falls, the crabs play hopscotch in sand,
While fireflies join in, oh isn't it grand?
With echoes of giggles, the island's alive,
Where humor shines bright, and good spirits thrive.

Shadows of Palms

The shadows of palms dance on the shore,
While lizards in top hats play games evermore.
A breeze whispers secrets, a tickle of fun,
As we chase the bright shadows 'til the day's done.

A parrot named Pete sings songs of delight,
He jokes with the tourists, 'You missed that last kite!'
Waves tickle our toes, we all giggle and greet,
That wobbly old crab who makes funny defeat.

Shells gather round for a sarcastic debate,
About who's the prettiest, the barnacle, mate?
It's laughter and noise that the sunset inspires,
As we toast to the ocean, and the humor it fires.

In this paradise, silliness reigns supreme,
With shadows and giggles like a wild, vivid dream.
Each moment a treasure, laughter swirling near,
In the warmth of the evening, we shed every fear.

Sunlit Waters

The sun sits high, it's a laugh-out-loud scene,
As splashing fish sing, 'We're the underwater keen!'
Flippers and fins twirl in a whimsical dance,
While dolphins make jokes, giving us all a chance.

A whale with a grin plays tag with the tide,
While a sea turtle winks, inviting us inside.
The starfish grumble softly, "Why are we out here?"
We all join the laughter, swimming with cheer.

In sunlit reflections, fun floats on the bay,
With mermaids quite cheeky, who swim in a play.
They tease with quick splashes, dive under the boat,
All while a crab wears a bright polka dot coat.

As the day passes by, the skies sparkle bright,
With each splash of laughter, more joy in our sight,
For sunlit waters bring giggles and glee,
In every sweet bubble, a wild jubilee!

Whispering Calypso

A tune in the air, oh how the rhythms flow,
With every soft whistle, we all sway to and fro.
The ukulele's strumming a comical beat,
As a chicken in shades tries to dance with two feet!

The island's alive with laughter and fun,
As the coconut juggler shows off in the sun.
Bananas join in, slipping all over the place,
While the locals just chuckle at the silly race.

A parrot named Louie claims he's the best,
"Just look at my feathers, they pass every test!"
But a goat with a grin stirs up quite the ruck,
With a hop and a skip, causing all kinds of luck.

Under twinkling stars, the calypso will soar,
As we laugh and we dance, wanting never to bore.
With jokes wrapped in melody, the night comes alive,
In whispers of fun, we happily dive.

The Heartbeat of the Coast

Seagulls squawk in awkward flight,
While crabs dance left, it's quite the sight.
The sunburnt tourists lose their hats,
Chasing waves like playful cats.

A beach ball bounces, wild and free,
Colliding with a palm tree's spree.
Children giggle, and sand sticks cling,
As a dog steals fries—it's a comical fling.

Sandy toes and ice cream stains,
Flip-flops flying, who needs reins?
A sunburned dad with sunscreen smeared,
His dance moves leave all amazed and weird.

The salty breeze gives hair a flair,
While beach umbrellas scatter everywhere.
In this chaos, joy insists,
Life's absurdity, we can't resist.

The Allure of Gentle Tides

Waves roll in with a gentle tease,
As surfers question, "Do we freeze?"
A picnic spreads, ants join the feast,
Sandwiches fly—thanks to a hungry beast.

A crab in shades walks by with pride,
While kids on boogie boards collide.
Sunscreen fights and laughter swell,
As someone yells, "Don't eat that shell!"

Seashells make a curious phone,
As seasick friends complain and moan.
The tide takes them where fun begins,
At least it's warm; just watch for fins!

Balloon animals float with style,
While beachside vendors sell with a smile.
In this parade of sun and cheer,
We find our joy, year after year.

Fragments of Paradise

Hammocks swing with groans and squeaks,
As sunbathers surrender to the peaks.
A coconut falls—watch your head!
While flip-flop fights break out instead.

The locals laugh with cheeky grins,
As tourists bumble in their sins.
Shell jewelry sparkles, what a steal!
But it's the conch shells that truly appeal.

A volleyball flies, it's in the air,
As laughter mingles with salty flair.
Ice cream cones drip down the line,
Someone's shirt? Now a colorful design!

A sunset paints the sky in hues,
While a parrot squawks the evening news.
With waves that dance, life seems so grand,
In this funny, warm, sandy land.

Heartstrings Tied to the Sea

Backflips are attempted, splashes fly,
As kids cry, "Just one more try!"
Sandy hairdos take a whole new form,
While jellyfish float—what a norm!

A fishing line tangled in the reeds,
As floppy hats become rare breeds.
An inflatable donut, now deflated,
Turns into laughter, quite underrated.

The ice cream truck plays an old tune,
While wise old turtles saunter, immune.
A hammock fight breaks with a squeal,
Who knew chaos could feel so real?

Magic nights where beachfires glowed,
Remember dances on the sand we strode.
With friendship wrapped in ocean breeze,
We find our peace with perfect ease.

Golden Hour Tranquility

The sun dips low, a cooling glow,
Crabs in sunglasses, put on a show.
Palm trees dance in a silly sway,
Fish gossip loudly about their day.

A parrot squawks, 'I want a drink!'
While iguanas pause to ponder and think.
Beach balls fly like a wild idea,
While kids burst into spontaneous cheer.

Laughter echoes with every wave,
Even the waves seem eager to rave.
Seashells chatter, they've secrets to tell,
Of mermaid parties and a clam's wish well.

As sun melts down, it's quite the sight,
Crickets start their disco tonight.
In this realm of skits and tales,
We're all the stars in life's funny trails.

Between Waves and Whispers

Between the waves, a turtle spins,
With a handsome grin, he stamps and wins.
Seashells giggle, shy yet bold,
Telling secrets of treasures untold.

A wave comes crashing—whoa, not again!
Sand between toes, it feels like a pen.
Crabs have a dance-off, oh what a sight,
Shaking their claws with all of their might.

Dolphins leap, tossing a ball,
As seagulls squawk of the summer's thrall.
Wet and wild with a comical flair,
Look out! A flip-flop flies through the air!

Beneath the sun, life's quite the show,
Surprises and laughter wherever you go.
In this beachy circus, all's good and bright,
Who knew nature's humor sparkled so light?

The Scent of Rainforest

In the jungle's heart, a monkey swings,
Chasing a cloud that giggles and sings.
Frogs in tuxedos hold a grand ball,
While vines play peek-a-boo, daring them all.

The rain drops down, a splashy surprise,
Umbrellas bloom in the sloth's sleepy eyes.
The air is thick with a syrupy tease,
A coconut smile floats down with ease.

Parrots barter, 'I'll trade you my squawk,
For a juicy berry, let's take a walk!'
Rain boots on, the ants march in line,
Chasing the thunder in rhythm and time.

Mossy carpets hide giggles and thrills,
While chattering roaches embrace their new skills.
In this fancier forest, so wild and spry,
Nature's humor always makes us sigh.

Twilight over Lagoon

When twilight tips its hat to the night,
Fireflies gather, oh what a sight!
The lagoon shimmers, as stories unfold,
Frogs in a choir sing ballads of gold.

Swans start their ballet, elegantly bright,
While turtles laugh at their awkward flight.
Cattails nod, they have tales to spill,
As the stars peek out and the moon's a thrill.

A raccoon sneaks snacks, a true gourmet,
While fish below plan a dance of display.
With splashes and giggles, the night comes alive,
In this world of whimsy, the fun will survive.

As the night deepens, the laughter won't cease,
In every ripple, we find our peace.
The lagoon, our stage, where we all belong,
Dancing through verses, we sing our song.

Melody of Sea and Sky

Seagulls dance and squawk so loud,
As I sip my drink, feeling quite proud.
The waves crash in a rhythmic beat,
Tickling my toes, what a bizarre treat!

Sun and cloud wear a silly grin,
Doing the cha-cha, where to begin?
Flip-flops flapping with every stride,
Beach balls bouncing, let giggles collide!

Crabs in their armor, patrolling the sand,
With sideways skitters, they silently stand.
I laugh as one tries to claim a towel,
While a rogue dog plots, giving a growl.

Laughter echoes through the bright blue day,
As friends stumble, trip, and sway.
In this carnival of sun and spray,
Life feels like a game, come out and play!

Voices of the Untamed Wilderness

In the jungle, a monkey swings so spry,
He steals my banana, oh my, oh my!
Squirrels chatter with a gossiping tone,
I can't help but giggle at their rambunctious zone.

A parrot squawks with flair and sass,
While I try to keep my lunch from grass.
Bears waltz by, tripping on their feet,
Who knew these creatures could be so sweet?

Vines stretch out like they're trying to hug,
I duck and roll from a playful bug.
Nature's carnival, oh what a show,
With each silly dance, my joy starts to grow!

The trees laugh softly, shaking their leaves,
As I leap around, trying to dodge the thieves.
Even the rocks seem to chuckle and smile,
In this wild wonder, let's linger awhile!

Enchanted Pathways

Wandering trails where the ferns wave high,
A lizard does yoga, under the sky.
I trip on a root, down I go,
Mushrooms giggle as they put on a show.

Butterflies flutter with a twirl and spin,
While bees buzz around with a typical grin.
The flowers gossip, their petals aflame,
As I ask the bugs, "Who's to blame?"

A squirrel in glasses reads a thick book,
Noticing me with a curious look.
I chuckle and wave, he doesn't reply,
Just flings a pinecone, oh my, oh my!

This path is alive, with laughter and cheer,
In every shadow, the whimsy draws near.
Let's dance with the breeze, let's frolic and play,
In nature's embrace, we'll brighten the day!

Blissful Horizons

Clouds like cotton candy drift overhead,
As my sandals squawk with every tread.
A hammock swings with a gentle sway,
While I snooze, dreaming of a brighter day.

The sun dips low, painting skies with flair,
I laugh as seagulls swoop down with a dare.
The glow of dusk, it tickles my toes,
With each burst of color, my happiness grows.

Jellyfish bob like balloons in a race,
While I try to keep up with the ocean's grace.
Dance like the waves, with a giggly shout,
Embrace every moment, there's fun all about!

Stars peek out, it's a mischievous night,
Fireflies twinkle, oh what a sight!
Join in this party, let laughter unfold,
In blissful horizons, let memories mold!

A Symphony of Leaves

A rustling orchestra in the trees,
Leaves play a tune with the lightest breeze.
The coconuts giggle, the palms sway and dance,
While lizards wear shades, caught in a trance.

An iguana strums on a bright ukulele,
While crickets keep time, a rhythm so frilly.
Swaying together, each branch takes a bow,
Nature's weird concert, come witness it now.

The sun sets low, and the beach chair sighs,
A pineapple's chuckle under playful skies.
Bananas wear hats that are big and round,
In the garden party, humor abounds.

Sun-Kissed Serenity

A coconut smiles at the ocean's foam,
While flip-flops dance, finding a home.
The seagulls hold court, with jokes in the air,
As beachgoers trip on their sun-kissed hair.

Sandcastles wobble, a royal decree,
That buckets of water shall flow endlessly.
With soggy sandwiches and laughter resound,
In this sun-soaked realm, joy knows no bound.

A squirrel in shades steals a fry from your plate,
While kids chase each other, it's quite the fate.
The sun rolls on down, giving nighttime a cue,
As fireflies giggle, like stars in the blue.

Breezes of Blue

The wind tells a story to kites in the sky,
While jellyfish wiggle and seagulls fly by.
A sandpiper struts, a comical sight,
Swapping jokes with a crab underneath the moonlight.

Umbrellas all spin as the gusts start to play,
While sunscreened tourists are caught in dismay.
A wave gives a splash, and the laughter erupts,
As flip-flops go flying, like popcorn erupts.

The old turtle chuckles from under a shell,
Each wave's a new joke, and all's going well.
Here under the sky, where mischief won't fade,
With breezes so blue, who needs a parade?

Reflections on Bougainvillea

Bougainvillea blushes in a bright display,
While bees in tuxedos come out to play.
The colors are vibrant, a crazy delight,
As butterflies caterwaul all through the night.

A florist misplaced all the plants in a spin,
Now flowers tell secrets to the bee with a grin.
They giggle and whisper through petals divine,
In a blooming confab that's utterly fine.

Sunlight dapples as the shadows do jig,
A garden soirée with a dancing twig.
Frogs in the corner wear crowns made of leaves,
While laughing at stories their best friend weaves.

Beneath the Canopy

Swinging high on a vine, with a grin,
A parrot laughed, let the fun begin.
Mangoes drop like cannonballs,
While lizards slide down tropical walls.

Monkeys throw coconuts, oh what a sight,
As they tumble, it's pure delight.
With every splash in the mud so deep,
Giggling creatures, not a soul can keep.

A sloth sips tea with careful flair,
While the sun spills in, with a bright glare.
Bamboo tickles, they squawk out loud,
Echoing laughter over the crowd.

Under the leaves, the dance goes on,
Fresh fruits rolling where smiles have drawn.
Beneath the canopy, life's a jest,
Nature's playground, we are truly blessed.

Serene Shores

On the beach, sand flies everywhere,
A crab scuttles off, without a care.
Laughter bubbles as waves collide,
Sunburned tourists try to hide.

Seagulls steal fries, they're very bold,
They swoop down quickly, oh so controlled.
Sun hats tumble and children squeal,
As the tide pulls back, with a funny reel.

Flip-flops float by in a splashy race,
While sunbathers try to find their place.
A beach ball bounces with silly glee,
As laughter dances across the sea.

Shells decorate toes, it's quite the display,
With every step, they wiggle away.
Serene shores hold mischief, it's true,
Bring on the giggles, the fun's never through.

Coral Dreams

Diving deep into a sea of cheer,
Fish in costumes, let's give a cheer!
A clownfish winks, doing ballet,
While a starfish juggles shells all day.

Coral castles with moat-like charm,
A shrimp is playing with great alarm.
As a turtle tiptoes, oh so slow,
We laugh as it trips on a seaweed throw.

Eels peek out, with a sly surprise,
Making faces with big, round eyes.
Bubbles giggle as they burst in air,
Coral dreams swirl with antics rare.

From anemones, the fun won't cease,
With every wave, there's a little peace.
Underneath the surface, laughter beams,
In this mad world of coral dreams.

A Dance of Tides

Once upon a coast, where sand meets foam,
A crab in a tuxedo feels right at home.
A sea star spins with disco flair,
While bouncing waves make the seagulls stare.

With every crest, the fish start to prance,
Octopus joins in for a wild dance.
Anemones wiggle with all their might,
As the moon smiles down, lending soft light.

The tide pulls back, oh what a sight,
Seashells play hide-and-seek in the night.
A dolphin leaps, making quite a fuss,
As the crowd of fish all join the bus.

The beach setting becomes quite the stage,
With flip-flops dancing, they're all the rage.
A dance of tides, where giggles collide,
In this playful water, let joy be your guide.

Nautical Reverie

A captain lost his rubber duck,
Sailing seas with all his luck.
A pirate's treasure map was there,
But all he found was seaweed hair.

He shouted loud, 'Where's my crew?'
But only seagulls laughed, it's true.
They squawked and danced on splashing waves,
While he just wished for sunny caves.

His compass spun, a dizzy ride,
And he forgot what's on the side.
The fish all giggled and swam in rings,
While he discussed his missing things.

So here's to sails that never cease,
And rubber ducks that bring us peace.
A nautical life, with humor bright,
Is better on a boat, alright!

Dancing Shadows at Dawn

As dawn broke through the sleepy night,
Dancing shadows took to flight.
A crab wore shoes and skittered fast,
While sunbeams twinkled, oh, what a blast!

The palm trees swayed in silly ways,
As monkeys joined in playful plays.
A parrot squawked some funny tunes,
While roosters danced beneath the moons.

With every leap, the sand would giggle,
And frolicking fish began to wiggle.
Beneath the sun's warm, golden brow,
The island life took a funny bow!

So let the shadows laugh and prance,
In the morning light, they find their chance.
With every chuckle from the breeze,
Life's a dance, so let's all freeze!

Whispers of the Island Spirit

On an island where rumors spread,
The coconuts all danced, it's said.
They whispered secrets to the trees,
About the guy who tripped on bees.

The spirits giggled in the air,
As someone fell and lost their hair.
A wave of laughter washed the shore,
And crabs exchanged a joke or four.

A little frog wore a fancy hat,
As tourists stumbled, imagine that!
They posed for pictures, all in a line,
While the tide rolled in, just in time.

So join the spirits, take a break,
In this land where laughs awake.
With every whisper, joy will bloom,
In this island's playful room!

Veiled in Ocean Mist

Veiled in mist, a mermaid sneezed,
Caught quite off guard by the breeze.
Her fin flapped wildly, what a sight,
As fishes chuckled with delight.

A treasure chest held nothing sweet,
Just old flip-flops and sticky feet.
The octopus played tag with the net,
And all the sea turtles looked quite upset.

A dolphin leaped but belly flopped,
And all the barnacles just stopped.
They laughed till waves rolled in their eyes,
In this mist where humor flies.

So dive into laughter, let it glide,
In the ocean's care, let joy abide.
With every splash, let giggles twist,
In this world veiled in ocean mist!

Symphony of the Whispering Palms

In vibrant hues, the sun did pop,
Coconuts swing like a comic flop.
Palms high-five with leaves in glee,
While crabs dance by, bold as can be.

A parrot squawks a silly tune,
While sea turtles slide like they're in a cartoon.
With flip-flops flapping, laughter flows,
As beach balls bounce where the seaweed grows.

Seagulls swoop, stealing fries,
As sunburnt folks chase after pies.
The rhythm of fun, a vibrant plight,
With sunburned noses and pure delight.

Under the shade, laughter spreads,
As sandcastles crumble like flying breads.
Each wave a wink, each splash a cheer,
In this joyful land, there's nothing to fear.

Glimpse of Heaven at Dusk

The sun's gone down, the stars are shy,
Fireflies twinkle, oh my, oh my!
A hammock swings with a lazy sway,
While crickets chirp a dance ballet.

Mangoes drop like comedy shows,
As we giggle at what nature throws.
With splashes of sunscreen on our nose,
We debate if that's a boat or a hose.

The moonlight winks, part of the jest,
As couples argue who's the best.
With ice cream cones and drippy sighs,
The evening's fun is no surprise.

Waves clap their hands on the soft sand,
As friends tell tales quite unplanned.
In this dusk glow, laughter's the key,
As the night hums its sweet melody.

Afterglow on the Shore

The sun's farewell paints the bay,
As beachgoers frolic in their own way.
Sand between toes, a giggling spree,
As waves chase down like a sprightly bee.

A beach ball flies, hits a sun hat,
While kids chase crabs, giving chatter a spat.
Seashells clatter in a giggling race,
As flip-flops dance with a joyful grace.

The sunset brings a funny cheer,
As someone trips and spills their beer.
Laughter echoes, the air so sweet,
In this afterglow, it's pure retreat.

Stars peep through like old friends do,
As shadows mingle, forming a crew.
Each wave's a punchline, splashing bright,
In this sandy paradise, hearts take flight.

The Essence of a Quiet Breeze

A gentle draft, like a prankster's sigh,
It teases the branches, makes them fly high.
With whispers of palm and giggles of light,
It swirls around, a fun-filled delight.

The scent of coconuts dances in air,
As sand slips through fingers without a care.
A playful gust gives a hat a new life,
As laughter erupts, cutting through strife.

Swaying hammocks hum a happy tune,
While sunburned folks melt under the moon.
The breeze carries tales of the sea's jest,
With jokes in the air, we're simply blessed.

Even the turtles seem to giggle,
As waves capsize on every little wiggle.
This quiet breeze, soft and free,
Whispers of laughter, just you and me.

The Lure of the Azure Abyss

Beneath the waves so deep and bright,
Fish wear hats, what a funny sight!
Coral reefs with smiles so wide,
Babbling currents, swaying side to side.

A sea turtle floats on a plank,
With a snorkel and a crazy prank.
Crabs in cliques, the king and jest,
They throw a dance-off, who's the best?

A dolphin juggles balls of sea,
While octopuses sip tea with glee.
Who knew the ocean's such a stage?
A splashy circus, in every page!

So next time you dive, don't be shy,
Join the fun with a wink and a fly.
For in this world of water's kiss,
It's all giggles, laughter, and bliss!

Cascading Colors of Twilight

As the sun sets, colors collide,
Pineapple juggling, what a ride!
Cocktail umbrellas dance in the breeze,
Sipping laughter, tasting tease.

The sky turns purple, clouds in sync,
Parrots gossip over a drink.
'Who wore it better?' they squawk and squint,
While flamingos strut, full of hint.

In the twilight, shadows twist and twirl,
An iguana's dance makes heads swirl.
Bamboo flutes play a cheeky tune,
As lizards rock, beneath the moon.

And in that moment, life's a jest,
Where joy and laughter come to rest.
So chase the colors till stars appear,
In this fun kingdom, let's cheer!

Secrets Beneath the Canopy

Monkeys chatter, plotting schemes,
Swinging through trees, chasing dreams.
A wise old sloth, with winks and grins,
Hides secrets where the laughter begins.

Leaves rustle with a giggling sound,
Squirrels playing tag, round and round.
A toucan with a beak so grand,
Shares tales of nuts from distant lands.

What's that rustling? Oh, a breeze!
Or maybe it's just a laughing sneeze.
With chattering crickets in full swing,
Nature's antics, what joy they bring!

So spill the beans, if you dare,
Join the critters, if you care.
For in this forest, fun abounds,
With laughter echoing all around!

Horizon's Embrace

As the sun peeks over the bay,
Seagulls squawk in a silly way.
A beach ball rolls, it goes astray,
Chasing crabs who can't help but play.

With sunscreen smears all over faces,
Beach lovers dance in funny places.
Children giggle, building tall towers,
While sandcastles bloom like floury flowers.

A dog in shades tries to surf,
Wipeout moments, oh, what a turf!
Flipping waves and splashes bright,
Each splash a giggle, pure delight.

So bask in joy, wherever you roam,
Find your laughter, call it home.
For on this shore, where fun meets grace,
Life is sweeter in horizon's embrace!

Celestial Ferns

In the jungle, ferns do twirl,
Grinning at each passing girl.
They whisper secrets, soft and green,
About the squirrels and their routine.

Cockatoos wear fancy hats,
Doing ballet with the bats.
The sun laughs and throws confetti,
While monkeys juggle, oh so petty!

Lizards slide on buttered rocks,
Chasing crickets, oh what shocks!
They giggle as they take a leap,
Into the pond, and make a beep.

With laughter echoing the trees,
The air is filled with buzz and keys.
Each vine a joke, each leaf a pun,
In this place, oh what fun!

Mirage of Paradise

Amidst the palms, a shimmer shows,
A beach, or is it just a pose?
I take a sip of coconut,
Then chase a crab that likes to strut.

Waves come in like surfing cats,
While seagulls wear their spiffy hats.
They squawk and dance, a feathery crew,
Sipping salty waves, how about you?

A flip-flop flies, a rogue retreat,
Lands on the head of a man so neat.
Laughter rolls like the waves nearby,
As swim trunks wave a heartfelt bye!

Under the sun's unyielding grin,
Even the breeze can't help but spin.
This mirage of joy, a sweet delight,
Where every day is a silly flight!

A Waltz with the Ocean

The ocean waltzes, kicks up foam,
While sea turtles glide elegantly home.
Clams join in, a clammy affair,
With a choreographed dance, quite rare!

Seashells tap in a joyful beat,
Crabs dressed up feel the heat.
A dolphin spins and takes a bow,
As fish flash colors, oh wow, wow!

Sun hats swirl with a breezy flair,
Partnered with the salty air.
In this dance, all worries flee,
As each wave sings its melody.

So come along, take a chance,
Join in this whimsical ocean dance.
With giggles tossed like fluffy clouds,
We'll waltz with the waves, all laughing loud!

Exotic Luminescence

Glowworms shimmer, stars in the night,
Jellyfish drift, glowing just right.
A party of colors fills the sky,
While toucans laugh and red birds fly.

Orchids giggle, wearing bright hats,
As frogs in bowties do acrobats.
Each fluttering leaf, a playful wink,
In this garden, mischiefs sync.

Nights filled with fireflies that tease,
Whispering secrets to the breeze.
The laughter of crickets fills the space,
While moonlit dances take their place.

In this glow of vibrant cheer,
Nature sings, come join us here!
With each twinkle and bright luminescent grace,
We'll jive in joy, a funny embrace!

When Sun Meets Sea

The sun slipped on some sunscreen, quite sublime,
While waves rolled in, doing flips in time.
Seagulls laughed at a crab's silly dance,
As flip-flops flew, in a wild romance.

A beachball landed on a fellow's head,
He looked surprised, then tripped on his tread.
The sandcastles crumbled, a sight so neat,
As kids squealed with joy, their summer retreat.

A hermit crab donned a shell from a shoe,
While sand dollars chuckled at the view.
The sun and sea shared a wink and a tease,
As laughter echoed through palm trees with ease.

With sunscreen wars and umbrellas that fight,
The sun met the sea, a comical sight.
Humor flows freely, like waves on the shore,
In a paradise where laughter's never a bore.

Nature's Gentle Embrace

A squirrel wearing glasses read a book,
While ants marched on, too busy to look.
The breeze chuckled softly, tickling leaves,
Nature whispered jokes, and everyone believes.

A turtle in shades was cruising so slow,
Wondering if he'd catch the summer show.
Flowers danced wildly, with petals like skirts,
Each one a comedian, cracking their flirts.

Birds were stand-up stars, with their own little plots,
Telling tales of worms that they had forgot.
The trees joined in, their branches swayed wide,
In a gentle embrace, where joy can't hide.

Nature's a circus, with a wild, warm heart,
Every critter and bloom plays its part.
In this funny show, we find our grins,
Where laughter and life are true wins.

Songs of Radiant Flora

The daisies composed a quirky little tune,
While violets chimed in, under the moon.
Roses wore sunglasses, all bloomed with flair,
While dandelions giggled, floating up in the air.

Sunflowers swayed, thinking they were stars,
Boasting about their yellow cars.
Lilies twirled, trying out some new moves,
Creating a rhythm—making everyone groove.

A berry bush blushed, feeling quite grand,
As bees buzzed in harmony, an orchestra band.
With petals as confetti, they danced through the night,
Creating a gala, a magical sight.

Nature's songs echo, in colors so bright,
In a garden of laughter, with pure delight.
Each blossom a comedian, each stem a fun cheer,
In this radiant garden, joy is always near.

Lanterns of the Night

Fireflies flickered, like disco balls,
Their glow illuminating the night's gentle calls.
Crickets crooned softly, a jazz band so slick,
While owls hooted rhythms—what a cool trick!

The moon made a joke about planes full of cheese,
While stars giggled back, in the cool evening breeze.
A raccoon in a mask, plotting his heist,
Scavenging snacks, oh, he lived so nice!

The shadows danced wildly, flipping about,
As lanterns of laughter lit up with no doubt.
A night full of stories, unfolding with glee,
Where each rustle and whisper sang tunes of esprit.

In this magical twilight, with humor in sight,
We laughed with the critters, on this joyful night.
With every soft flicker, the world came alive,
In the lanterns of laughter, our spirits will thrive.

Echoes in the Mangroves

In swaying trees, a parrot chats,
Sipping nectar, wearing hats.
A turtle wearing shades, so cool,
Waves hello—he's nobody's fool.

The crabs are dancing in a line,
Doing the conga, oh so fine!
A fish in flip-flops makes a splash,
While mermaids giggle, making a dash.

Rain drums down on a muddy floor,
Slippers sliding, what's in store?
A froggy slips, oh what a sight,
Jumping back up, feeling just right.

Bamboo rattles, reggae plays,
The scene unfolds in sunny rays.
Nature's laughter fills the air,
In mangrove echoes, joy to share.

The Pulse of Nature

The sun's a thief, it steals the day,
While iguanas scheme in their own way.
A monkey's juggling berries with flair,
Laughter ripples everywhere.

Seashells whisper, telling tales,
While the wind plays tricks with sails.
A pelican falls, trying to dive,
It fumbles but hops back, oh so alive!

The breeze does a shimmy, oh what fun,
Tickles the palm trees, one by one.
A lazy hammock, sways with glee,
While parrots tease from coconut trees.

Bees buzz in a jazzy tune,
Chasing flowers under the moon.
Nature's pulse, a heartbeat loud,
In this funny realm, we're all so proud.

Driftwood Dreams

A log turned boat, a pirate's throne,
Sailing seas, where no one's flown.
A crab with a compass, leads the way,
But he's lost, oh what a display!

A dolphin flips—does it know the score?
Mischievous fish at the ocean's door.
A clam snaps shut, oh what a pout,
As starfish giggle, in and out.

The tide rolls in with a lawyer's claim,
For lost items cast from the game.
A seashell chorus sings with cheer,
While driftwood dreams float ever near.

In this watery world of wonder,
Life's a joke—laugh, it's a thunder!
Joyful waves crash, swirl around,
In driftwood dreams, humor's found.

Seeds of Serenity

In the garden, a squirrel plays,
Scattering seeds in funny ways.
A flower sneezes, pollen's spread,
While bees buzz around its head.

A cucumber dreams of being a star,
While chatting with radishes from afar.
The soil giggles under a sunbeam,
As worms wiggle in their mud-themed dream.

The corn stalks dance a jig so nice,
While grabby hands try to entice.
Tomatoes blushing, oh what a sight,
Running away, avoiding the bite.

Laughing leaves in a breezy beat,
Nature's humor never to retreat.
In a patch of joy, you'll likely find,
Seeds of glee, the best kind!

www.ingramcontent.com/pod-product-compliance
Lightning Source LLC
Chambersburg PA
CBHW072128070526
44585CB00016B/1574